Table of Contents

Introduction 2
Universal Basic Income Explained 3
Social Programs 5
The Problems with UBI Experiments 6
Understanding the Social Class War 7
    The Lower Class 8
    The Middle Class 9
    The Upper Class 10
Automation Will Eliminate Jobs 11
People will stop working 12
UBI is Expensive 13
Taxes 14
UBI-Socialist System 15
Age of UBI Beneficiaries 16
Top up Feature 17
The Rich 19
Less crime 20
Reduced Poverty 21
Increased jobs 22
Inflation 23
UBI Monthly Amount 24
In the End 25
Thanks 26

Introduction

Universal Basic Income offers a solution to many of our social and economic challenges. This book addresses several misconceptions about UBI and showcases the issues concerning UBI and their solutions.

An economy where everyone is able to live comfortably and no poverty exists is achievable and UBI is one of the solutions in achieving this.

This book introduces several issues and their solution along with the benefits of UBI

Universal Basic Income Explained

Universal Basic Income is periodic payments made to permanent residents/citizens of a country without any requirements outside of age. It's recommended to pay enough to meet the individual's basic needs. There have been several experiments over the years to show the impact of UBI however it's yet to break free of the experimental stage.

Despite the challenges, it is seen as an idea to consolidate other welfare programs such as unemployment insurance as it provides a stable income while protecting workers during a downturn while eliminating poverty and creating a better standard of living.

It is also seen as a way to boost the economy and by extension businesses as they will receive more clients and increased sales.

Linking UBI to Income

Some countries may choose to link the income salary to the amount they pay to UBI recipients. Though well intentioned, this is not a good policy as it creates a situation where some persons are not motivated to work. The amount paid should be the same regardless of the income of the individual.

Politically, this may be an easier option but it's not the right policy and countries should avoid this potentially disastrous policy.

If UBI pays up to $1000 per month and you are working $800 then your UBI pays $200. It also means that persons working over $1000 will not get any payments. This is a demotivation for persons working below $1000 as their income will be the same regardless if they are working or not. For those who may be working $1100, they may choose to stop working and lose that extra $100 than continue working for an extra $100.

If on the other hand, you get $1000 regardless of income, you would be taking home $1800 in this same situation. This creates a motivation to work and contribute to society without losing any benefits. The person making $1100 will now be making $2100.

Care must be taken to ensure that all individuals are benefiting and it doesn't create a disincentive to work or appear unfair to one set of individuals.

Social Programs

Some countries can pay for UBI and maintain all social programs and kudos to them. However, most countries don't have that luxury and will be forced to resort to increased borrowing or taxes to pay for this program if done as an additional benefit.

Increased borrowing is not sustainable; it creates an economic spiral that may collapse the economy. Although the increased spending may boost tax receipt, it is usually not enough to counteract increased debt.

Hardly anyone wants increased taxes. Increased taxes even for well-intended purposes can be damaging. Increased taxes shouldn't fund non capital recurring expenditures.

It's important that the government seeks to get the majority of all income to fund the UBI by cutting expenses in its social programs and lastly privatize some government entities in a financially responsible way.

One method is by creating a sovereign wealth fund and using it's dividends to assist in maintaining the program. Instead of selling an asset completely, maintain shares in the entity or even better yet, maintain 100% of the business while running it as a profit generating business

The Problems with UBI Experiments

The first problem is that it's an experiment. While you may get an understanding of how UBI may work in real life, you have to also remember that the data isn't always accurate.

You are working $1200 monthly and you are one of the beneficiaries of an UBI experiment that pays $1000 per month for 1 year. Would your decisions on spending be different if it was for 30 years vs. 1 year? For most, it would affect your decisions therefore your validity of the data.

Most experiments don't measure the impact on businesses and government revenues as its impact is usually too small to notice.

That $1000 can be spent at a local grocery store, a few items at the market etc. This is additional revenue going to these businesses and also additional taxes to the government...

To truly determine if UBI is suitable is to implement it in a closed loop system within a subset of a country such as a state. This allows the GDP, effect on taxation etc. to be properly measured and not just the impact on a few 100 individuals.

Understanding the Social Class War

One of the major challenges with the implementation of UBI isn't politicians or even its feasibility but it's the same beneficiaries themselves. Looking at UBI through the lens of the different classes is very interesting. They all say that UBI should be implemented and they should benefit however there seems to be an issue with the other social classes benefiting. While there is increasing agreement from the different social classes to its implementation, it continues to be the major impediment.

It's believed that once implemented, there wouldn't be much resistance once the choice is complete discontinuation or continuation of the program as most individuals wouldn't want the program to end.

The Lower Class

They want UBI because they do some of the hardest work with the least pay. They are the types that work in fast food restaurants, farms etc. If they miss a paycheck, it's like the world is coming to an end. Surely, they are deserving of UBI as this would make life a lot easier for them and raise their standard of living. This class also tends to live either below or near the poverty line.

But when asked, if others should benefit, they are against those more fortunate benefiting as they feel that they haven't done anything to deserve it and that they don't need it. They usually ask that the entire money should just be shared with them alone.

The Middle Class

They want UBI because they pay the most taxes as a percentage of their income and believe they should be getting back some of that money. They also say that they would spend it more responsibly than others. They usually just make enough to live a decent life however a single event can bring them into the lower class.

They are against the poor receiving it because they view them as wasteful with their money and that they may stop working and collect free money while they will continue having to deal with their challenging jobs. They also believe that the lower class don't work hard enough or sacrifice enough why they are still in that position.

The Upper Class

They wants those below them to have enough of a decent life to prevent them from envying them or wanting to take away their riches. They also see it as a way to make up their excessive wealth.

They fear that UBI may result in more taxes and make it harder for them to find staff willing to work for them doing personal tasks since they are already receiving a decent income.

Many individuals are already benefiting from government funding via social programs, UBI is just a method of distribution which reduces bureaucracy and creates economic growth.

Automation Will Eliminate Jobs

The robots are coming for your jobs. From the beginning of the industrial revolution, we have been hearing that machinery or technology will leave very few jobs for us. It's true that jobs will be lost to automation but history has shown us that not only new jobs will be created but even more than before.

Jobs are always evolving. A lot of jobs that exist now didn't exist 50 years ago and some jobs haven't even been created yet. Yes, innovation may eliminate some jobs and force us to retrain for new jobs or create our own business. I know that it's not easy when you train yourself in one area only to be told, you need to retrain for a new area but this is the path we must all follow.

UBI helps as it will provide a stable income allowing that individual to retrain and take up a new career instead of worrying where the next meal will come from. Maybe one day, we will all be jobless but I wouldn't think too hard on that one as we always find new ways to survive.

People will stop working

Ask yourself, would you stop working if you received UBI? Most people want to accomplish things and won't stop working even if they can cover their basic expenses. Stop thinking you are smarter than others because others are saying the same thing.

When you see someone who is no longer poor starts earning a better income, do they stop working or do they try to increase their income. Yes, there are some who may temporarily stop working but once they see their friends and family buy things they want, they will fall in line.

Plus if most of your friends are at work while you stay at home, you will get bored eventually. That also goes for even the richest amongst us, they find other activities to occupy themselves.

What may change slightly is that the wage for some low income jobs may increase since more persons will try to find better paying jobs instead of running into the first job they receive.

UBI is Expensive

The government is already spending a significant amount of its budget on social programs; UBI simply converts it into a single program. UBI will be cheaper as it's more simplified and eliminates bureaucracy and all the staff required to run all the different programs.

If the country doesn't have the necessary infrastructure before such as all individuals and businesses being registered and appropriate data management then it may be expensive to initially launch the program.

However once successfully implemented, it should run smoothly without much intervention from the government. The country's business model may need to change to get the best out of the program such as the use of consumption tax.

Taxes

The idea is the elimination of most or all other Government programs and redirecting funds to cover the UBI.

UBI will result in more consumers having an income. This means they would spend more. That increased spending will boost revenue for businesses. That increased revenue will boost the taxes they pay over to the government.

Businesses typically try to ensure that their staff ratio is in line with the volume of transactions/customers they have to prevent extended wait time. UBI will increase both of these measures and businesses will hire more persons. This would increase payroll taxes to the government.

An increase in income and expenditure by an individual or business usually has a multiplier effect as it increases income for another individual or business. This income is also taxable and thus increases government revenues.

The Government will be able to increase or decrease its payout to avoid increasing taxes to pay for the program.

Tax reform is also another method to ensure the right taxes and ratio is applied to ensure its success.

Considering this, UBI could result in the government revenue increasing while taxation is either lowered or remains the same but there should be no need for an increased taxation rate.

UBI-Socialist System

There is no such thing as free money and UBI understands this; which is why UBI proposes the elimination of other programs and adjustments to taxes to pay for this program. So it's not an increase in government expenses. In fact, it can result in less government expenses.

Money in UBI is taking money from one source to another with the aim of advancing a country's residence in an efficient way. This is currently happening via taxes and existing welfare programs.

UBI also calls for the privatization of existing government entities in a fiscal responsible method.

Some may see this as a social program, however UBI will actually increase capitalism as more persons will enter business, create more private sector jobs and it will significantly reduce the size of the government.

If the government eliminates most or all social programs, then the size of the public sector would reduce significantly. UBI is one single payment to everyone so that would require much less staff.

UBI provides income to individuals to buy more. Increased income will encourage businesses to increase staff and more persons will want to open businesses.

So the government will employ less persons and be less involved in activities in the country.

Does this sound like socialism or capitalism?

Age of UBI Beneficiaries

One of the challenges with UBI is determining who should get the monthly payment. There are 3 categories to consider; under 18 18 to pensionable age and pension age.

One of the reasons in favor of individuals under 18 receiving UBI is the need to support children especially if the parents are poor with more children than they can financially support.

On the other hand, if money is distributed to each child in which the parents would ultimately be in charge of spending, it could create a motivation for individuals to have children so they can get access to extra money.

The solution varies depending on the needs of the country. Some may wish to increase their population while others may want to decrease it. It's important to consider if giving children money is ideal based on your country's goals and financial ability.

Individuals age 18 to pension age are typically the best candidates to receive UBI due to their need to spend and their contribution to economic growth.

Some countries may merge pension payments into UBI however this should be carefully considered. If pension payments are being rolled into UBI, governments need to ensure that affordable insurance exists to ensure pensioners are not hit with any high expenses.

They also need to be aware that unlike working age individuals, pensioners don't usually have any additional income. It's recommended that a portion of the UBI received can be transferred to a savings account in addition to a higher UBI if possible.

Top up Feature

One of the benefits of UBI is the ability to increase spending. However if a significant portion of the population decides to save the money received then it would make the program more expensive. Countries should resist depositing money directly into an individual's account and hoping they spend it.

To achieve the desired result, it's important that a top up feature is used for payment as it's the most effective method. The top up feature works by ensuring that any unused sum is carried over to the next period and the government would only provide the difference to make up the amount payable for the UBI.

By choosing this option, it forces individuals to spend the money they receive otherwise it's gone. This helps to boost the economy and generate tax revenue for the government making the program more cost effective.

It also means because not everyone will use their entire portion, it would save the government additional sums of money making it even more cost effective than direct payments to an account which can't be recovered easily.

Individuals can receive their UBI payments via a card specifically designed to facilitate the top up feature or an app or any other secure payment system which would allow a top up functionality.

Where to Spend UBI

UBI helps in improving consumers spending ability however if it's being spent in another country, it won't be helpful for the local economy. Businesses are the backbone of most countries as they provide a significant portion of tax payments in most countries. It's recommended that the usage of UBI payments be limited to the businesses in the country.

By restricting its use exclusively to the local economy, it will boost local businesses to allow them to grow and gain new clients. It will also increase taxes payable to the government via the multiplier effect.

Some countries may choose to restrict large multinational companies from being one of the businesses who can receive payment from the program or restrict certain types of businesses however this should be avoided as it may hurt investment in the country.

What should be implemented is the right taxation on sales, profit and dividends.

The Rich

One of the most contentious groups who will receive UBI payments are the super-rich. Even most or all of them agree that they shouldn't be receiving the money. However, if we were to create a bureaucratic system to prevent those that are more fortunate to not receive payments, we may find that cost is usually more than what they would receive.

There are several ways in how the program is set up to allow those most fortunate not to be beneficiaries and so provide even more funds for others.

The government can simply use an opt-out function whereby they can choose to be removed from the list of beneficiaries of UBI payments. .

The recipients can choose not to spend the money as it's a top feature used for payment thereby no more than the initial payment will ever go to the card.

A more open method is for a list of persons who didn't use their UBI payment in any given period to be publicly available. However this should be avoided as it can be embarrassing especially for those who normally can afford it however due to a particular circumstance in a month, they require extra money. At the same time, it can be used as a public thank you to those that didn't use their payment.

Less crime

Crimes occur for varying reasons however one of the major reasons is due to the need to survive. Some individuals simply don't have an adequate income source to pay for food etc and use crime to supplement this.

While not every poor person commits crime, it does play a role. When you give someone the option of either feeding their child by stealing a few items in a grocery store or watching my child die of hunger, not many would choose to let their child die.

If you have your basic needs being met, you are less motivated to be involved in crimes. Increased income usually leads to more job opportunities and employed individuals are less likely to commit crimes.

Decreasing crime boosts the economy as businesses no longer have to spend so much money on security measures. Businesses wouldn't have to raise prices to compensate for stolen items. Individuals will be able to shop more without the constraints of worrying about being mugged etc

Even if you aren't in favor of UBI, wouldn't you consider it just based on being safer and having desperate parents who just want to feed their family?

Reduced Poverty

One of the benefits of UBI is that it provides an income sufficient to ensure poverty can be easily eliminated. Every night, millions of individuals go to their bed without even a single meal.

However with UBI, everyone is earning a minimum income and it affords them the ability to pay for items such as food. UBI will not cure all financial problems amongst the poor but it creates a base that will make it easier to lift them out of poverty.

No government wants to know that their citizens are living in poverty needlessly. It is also more costly to take care of the poor as their health is usually worse than those who can afford better food and health care.

The world has been trying to eliminate poverty and UBI is one of the best tools to accomplish this.

Increased jobs

One of the benefits of UBI is an increased number of persons who receive constant monthly income. Those persons now have 1 month to spend that money. This means business income will increase significantly. With increased consumption, businesses may increase staff to meet the demand.

One of the effects of more consumers is that persons may decide to start their own business. This means they may have to hire more workers and the cycle continues.

With increased focus on private enterprises, it would create more competition from an increased number of businesses and thus more individuals will be hired.

Inflation

With increased income, there is usually a pressure of increased inflation which negatively affects the buying power of salary received. This is a major issue as it can make things worse especially for the poor.

UBI, once implemented mostly with the same money that was being spent on social programs in addition to appropriate taxation, should reduce the likelihood of high inflation.

More individuals are expected to start businesses; the increased competition should create a downward pressure on inflation as businesses compete for the same customers.

UBI Monthly Amount

What should be the monthly payment for UBI? There isn't a straightforward answer as every country will differ. It should however be at least at or above the poverty line.

A quick calculation would be to get together the budget of all the social programs that will be eliminated and divide it by the number of citizens above 18 and add 20% to the amount.

The amount paid can be tweaked monthly based on income and expenditure of the government of the previous month however a minimum figure must be set. By adjusting the monthly amount paid, the government can compensate based on its finances and various macro-economic circumstances. It's also expected not everyone will spend their allotment each month.

In the End

At the end of the day, the benefits of Universal Basic Income outweigh the negatives and it will take political will to get such legislation done. The variables can be significant however I believe this guide will avoid failure of such a system.

We must start with individuals demanding such a system and once it gains enough traction then politicians will be more motivated to implement the concept. Once implemented, there should be no going back which is why it's success is so important.

I hope this provides a guide to answer questions about the program and how to promote its benefits. I didn't directly present the negatives as if you approach it from how the concept works, then it automatically solves any negatives.

At times, we pull down each other as we believe that only ourselves should excel, not realizing that you will succeed more in life if we help each other to grow.

Thanks

Universal Basic Income has been proposed over the years by several individuals who have poured their heart and mind in trying to get it being a government policy. Several entities have done experiments over the years to showcase the benefits of UBI. A number of documentaries have been made and books have been written.

I thank everyone for promoting UBI in their own unique way as we aim to create a better life and eliminate poverty across the world.

Support Universal Basic Income

www.ingramcontent.com/pod-product-compliance
Lightning Source LLC
Chambersburg PA
CBHW080440220526
45465CB00009B/3363